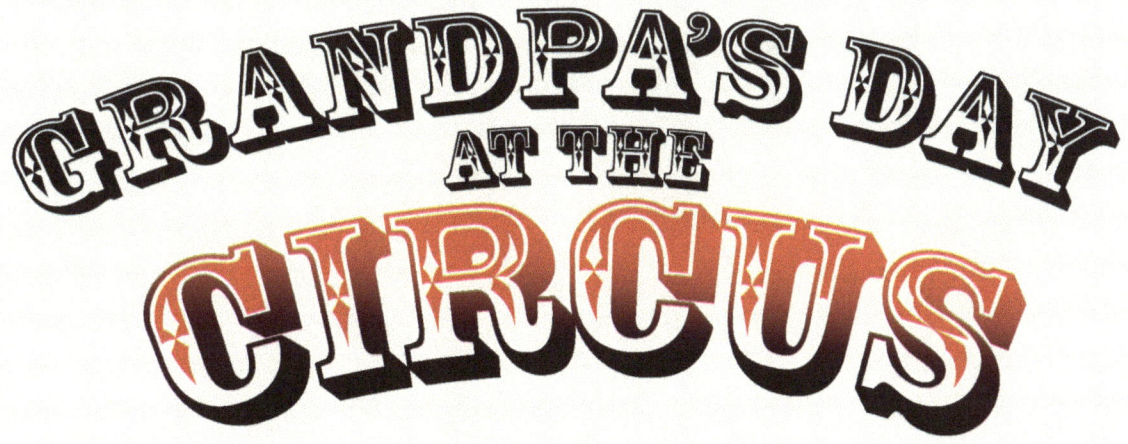

Grandpa's Day at the Circus

J. William Zoldak

Illustrations by Misti Feliciano Hobbs

DEDICATION

In honor of Tiny and the thousands of other circus workers who brought joy to generations of children and adults across America.

Grandpa's Day at the Circus
J. William Zoldak

FIRST EDITION

Hardcover ISBN: 9781087980102
Softcover ISBN: 9781087980898

ALL RIGHTS RESERVED.

©2021 J. William Zoldak
Illustrations by Misti Feliciano Hobbs.

No part of this publication may be translated, reproduced or transmitted in any form without prior permission in writing from the publisher.

Published by Stonehedges
OXFORD, MASSACHUSETTS

Dear Grandchildren,

I know that in the not too distant past some of you attended the Ringling Brothers Circus as part of its farewell tour. I'm glad that you had a chance to experience "The Greatest Show on Earth" before it passed away into history. I'm reminded of an experience that I had as a young boy with the circus, many years ago in the 1950's. I would like to share that experience with you in this letter.

The circus would come to our town periodically as part of its yearly circuit. It didn't come every year, but when it did, there was always great excitement throughout the community. The time that I remember occurred in a section of our town called Firthcliff in a large open field that no longer exists. Firthcliff was about a mile from my grandmother's house and a place that I knew well. The field was owned by the carpet company that was located there. I assume the circus was arranged by the company for the enjoyment of the town. The Firth Carpet Company was the largest employer in our town.

I had heard that the circus would sometimes hire local kids to help with the set up and would pay them by giving them free tickets to the show that night. As a boy of twelve, this really appealed to me. So, I got up early on the day that the circus was expected to be in town and walked over to see if I could get a job.

When I arrived, I found the field full of trucks, wagons, all kinds of animals and circus people. Because this was my first time experiencing this, I didn't know how to go about getting a job. So, I walked around bewildered. There seemed to be different areas of the circus set up in some kind of loose order. In one large area there were workers rolling out what turned out to be a huge tent (the Big Top), using elephants to move the equipment around and carrying the heavy poles.

I recognized several kids who were among the helpers and wondered how they got their jobs. By the time I got around to asking, I was told that no more help was needed setting up the tent. Not knowing what to do, I simply wandered around asking if anyone needed help.

Finally, I passed a place where there were several horses (perhaps eight or ten of them) all grayish blue in color and tied up next to a trailer and eating hay. There were a couple of men tending the horses. I walked up to one of them and asked if I could help them. Because I was familiar with horses and had worked at a stable since I was 8 years old, I hoped they might consider me.

To my surprise, a man named Tiny (he was quite the opposite) said yes. I was overjoyed and spent the next few hours feeding, cleaning and brushing these beautiful animals. They were called Liberty Horses, a term that I didn't know until years later meant that they were horses that were specially chosen and trained to do tricks in response to voice commands. I, of course, knew none of that at the time. I only knew that I was accepted for the job.

After most of the work was done, I sat with Tiny and the other men talking and joking around. The men took turns sharing experiences and boasting about things that they had done or were able to do. For example, at one point Tiny grabbed a sledge hammer and started doing a trick. He held the hammer out straight with one hand and then he tipped the heavy head of the hammer back toward his face. As it got closer to his face, he slowed his motion down to bring it to the end of his nose. After touching his nose, he slowly raised it back again. I was sure that his strength would give out and he would hit himself in the face but he never did. He then handed me the hammer and asked me if I would like to try. I emphatically declined. Over the next few years, however, I did try to do it, and eventually, with a lot of practice, accomplished it.

Just before lunch time, I asked Tiny if I would be able to get a free ticket to the circus that night. He told me not to worry because he would get me in when the time came. I then ran to my grandmother's house for lunch. After eating quickly, I returned to the circus. My grandmother packed me some sandwiches to have for supper, so that I didn't have to leave the circus again before the show.

When I returned, Tiny and the other men were still relaxing, but as time went on, they started preparing for the show that night. At one point Tiny asked one of the other men if he thought a particular horse needed new shoes. When the man said yes, they decided to get it done immediately because show time was approaching rapidly.

They then did something that I had never heard of before or since, but I swear it happened right in front of my eyes. Both men worked on the horse at the same time. Tiny worked on the right rear hoof at the same time that the other man worked on the left front hoof. Each man leaned into the horse, balancing the horse while it stood on only the other two feet. They then switched feet and did it again. The horse had four new shoes in record time. I was amazed, as were the other people who saw it. When I asked Tiny if he had ever done that before, he said no, but that he always wondered if he could.

Just before the circus was to begin, I asked Tiny again about getting a seat for the show. He said that he might need my help because one of the men that was supposed to lead the horses into the ring hadn't arrived yet. I told him that I would be happy to help. He then brought me into the circus, through the performers entrance, to a front row seat. It was probably the best seat in the tent. Part way through the show, he came back to tell me that the man had finally arrived so I didn't have to lead the horses in after all.

I enjoyed the show greatly, but I must say, I do wish the man had not shown up so that I could tell you that your grandfather once led the Liberty Horses into the ring at one of the greatest shows on earth. I do say, however, that it was a wonderful experience and one that I will never forget.

Well, that's my circus story. The next day the circus moved on to the next town, and I never saw Tiny or the Liberty Horses again, but, oh, what a great memory! The Big Top, the wild animals, the clowns, the elephants, the trapeze artists, all the other acts, and, of course, the Liberty Horses have now moved on into history, but that day lives on within me.

You, too, will have wonderful unexpected experiences in your life that you will cherish. Hold on to them and share them because each time you do, they will enrich your life over and over again. I can assure you that, while I only spent one day with Tiny, I think of him often and as a special friend.

Love as always,

Grandpa

www.ingramcontent.com/pod-product-compliance
Lightning Source LLC
Chambersburg PA
CBHW061150010526
44118CB00026B/2931